HIRAETH

POEMS BY
CAROL ROSE DANIELS

inanna poetry & fiction series

INANNA Publications and Education Inc.
Toronto, Canada

The publisher gratefully acknowledges the support of the Canada Council for the Arts and the Ontario Arts Council for its publishing program. The publisher is also grateful for the financial assistance received from the Government of Canada..

Cover artwork: Carol Rose Daniels, "Feels Like Home," 2017, mixed media with acrylic on canvas, 48 x 36 inches.

Cover design: Val Fullard

Library and Archives Canada Cataloguing in Publication

Daniels, Carol, 1963–, author
        Hiraeth / Carol Rose Daniels.

(Inanna poetry & fiction series)
Poems.
Issued in print and electronic formats.
ISBN 978-1-77133-485-3 (softcover).— ISBN 978-1-77133-486-0 (epub).—
ISBN 978-1-77133-487-7 (Kindle).— ISBN 978-1-77133-488-4 (pdf)

        I. Title. II. Series: Inanna poetry and fiction series

PS8607.A5567H57 2018   C811'.6   C2018-901521-7
                                                           C2018-901522-5

Printed and bound in Canada

Inanna Publications and Education Inc.
210 Founders College, York University
4700 Keele Street, Toronto, Ontario M3J 1P3 Canada
Telephone: (416) 736–5356   Fax (416) 736–5765
Email: inanna.publications@inanna.ca Website: www.inanna.ca

MIX
Paper from
responsible sources
FSC® C004071

This book is dedicated to the memory of my beautiful Rose.
Until we meet again my little one.

Contents

KOOKUM (*spirit wisdom*)

hiraeth – pron. (HERE – eyeth)

> (n.) a homesickness for a home to which
> you cannot return, a home which maybe never was;
> the nostalgia, the yearning, the grief for the
> lost places of your past.

THE LITTLE PEOPLE (*helpers*)

spirit beings — assigned by Creator —
primarily to children
to ensure their safety and well-being

Unravelling Threads

Call yourself a mother?

yet
could never bring yourself
to hold
this little brown hand
in public

always qualifying
with the words

she's adopted

spoken hurriedly
ashamedly

What will the neighbours think?

oh they better watch out
those Indians are nothing but trouble
will probably be hooker by the time she's 12
don't let your kids play with her
she probably has lice   they all do you know

no childhood should know
too many fist fights
trying to erase
the shameful word of squaw

while you sit on the sidelines

years later
I hear the drum
out of your reach
you have no control
it touches that beautiful part of my soul

a place where your cracks begin to show
and all the lies you told me have to go

I am brown
a Cree and proud
I sing strong
you cover your ears
to a truth
you do not want to hear

I am tired of pretending to be
someone I am not

I have found my spirit

and move forward
to the place I belong
away from your noise
and into the song

I shall dance

Spellbound

Purple chiffon flowing
dancing to a yellow moon
calling to invoke
laughter

Your expression
dour too long

Whispering
coaxing
a change of heart
that still flows
red with anger

Filthy Cloak

Shame
forced to wear this filthy cloak
burdens each day
of childhood

made of velcro
lies stick like flies
names singe the soul
ugly
to be brown

Times change
so do hearts
as fear wanes
and pride gains

Time has allowed me
to now disrobe
in public
and force the shame back where it came from

you wear this filthy thing in public
your ideas
always filled with
the blackness of this robe

Sunday

Laying out white socks
crisp and clean
as if it will cover your heart
hard and mean

get ready for church
repent and pray
pretend to be kind
on Sunday

The neighbours watch
the priest is there
pretend and smile
as if you care

After the service
parishioners gone
I don my rags
continue a song of woe

but not forever
I know
someday soon
I will grow
away from you

Ravens Crossed at Midnight

Ravens are old   cunning   wise
stealing when the sun is high
they do not fly
at night

If you see this
turn back

Why?

Raven foreshadows doom in black sky
Listen

Ravens do not fly at night
neither do I

Flight

Life cannot be
all rage and madness and sadness
surround yourself with guilt
spirit wilts

surround with light
magic takes flight

destination unknown
but wishing for cold winds to drift me away

no longer stuck between two worlds
belonging to neither

Ugly squaw   go back where you came from
Apple   you act like a monias

I am no ugly squaw
I am beautiful   *Iskwew*
and
I shall never be white
except for my thoughts
pure and light

is the reason I pray

dance at full moon
eat bannock in bed

helping ignore what others have said
stamp out all doubts that get in the way
tell Creator I am thankful to greet each new day

what ever it may hold

Kinanaskomitin

Qu'Appelle?

Racist uncle knocks at the screen door
it is made of old wood
used to be part of a barn
torn down years ago after being damaged by wicked winds
seemingly ever present

Daddy answers
Hey what's up? Just put on a pot
come on in

the discussion with his older brother?
amicable
for a while

gas prices are up
sure could use some rain already
did you know you can make soup from rhubarb?

small talk comes to an abrupt end
as racist uncle
foolishly ventures towards places forbidden
the off-limits

Not still thinking about adopting that schwartze   I hope?
Don't call her that
No, I'm serious   you are only asking for trouble.
I am warning you drop it

Be reasonable, I know she is like a pet to you   but really.
She is my daughter   you arse
She's an Indian.
That doesn't matter
What the hell?   There is no need for you to take her in like this.
For Christ sake   even her own mother got rid of her.
I am warning you.   Stop talking.   Apologize for that.
This is my daughter you are saying these things about
I'm not apologizing for anything.   Shit!   What's wrong with you?
Defending a goddam little Indian   for Christ sakes?

Eavesdropping
this exchange
that lasts less than one minute
but damages me
for a lifetime

Okay that is it.   If you cannot say anything nice then get the hell out of
my house   and don't come back until you can apologize!

A slam of fists atop a round formica table
cold coffee splashing to mark the spot
mark the day

racist uncle wears a look of shock
defeated
love trumps

he slowly walks out the old wooden door

never visits our house again

It is the first of many times I remember
Daddy stepping in
sheltering me from the harm and the hatred

I never got a chance to say
thank you
for carrying me on your shoulders
lifting me out of those battles

a raging war where I never enlisted
but found myself living

I also thank Creator for showing me
love is colour blind
so was Daddy
ever my hero
never remaining silent
in times of need

I miss him

Rest in peace
winged warrior
I will tell good stories about you

Lesson

It is morning
dog goes outside

sipping coffee
I forget about her
until a scratching at the door
beckons

If door was not closed tight
she would push it open
and let herself in

A lesson in faith

It is going to happen

that door will open
when the time is right

Patience

it's why I do beadwork

Leftovers

I love my turkey soup
things left over
repurposed
and made anew

taking the same ingredients
reworking them

similar outcome
but unique unto itself

like love

I love my turkey soup
this time
stirred in with care
gently flavoured
but not too many spices

it is going to be good
like the family and friends
who enjoy a big bowl

I love my turkey soup
because it makes you smile
and that makes me happy

Grandmother Moon

Grandmother Moon speak to me
to help understand things unseen
the sound of faerie voices
the Church calls it evil
it says the same about my people

like when I burn some sage
and say a prayer
get sent to confession
with rosary and veil

It is all so confusing
to be told I am wrong
the main reason
because I am brown

Grandmother Moon
help me to know
goodness and truth come from within
and that the Church is wrong
to call me a sinner

Stop all the noise
they plant in my head

they say our women are wicked
and so are our songs
they say everything about my people is wrong

I am
only five
too small to argue
too small to fight

Grandmother Moon help
nourish this spirit
before it is a shell
help me be brave and defiant
keep me well

keep me strong enough to walk alone
until such time
I can come home

My Secret Hiding Spot

You are where I go
when others
no longer able to hide the rot
within that stench-ridden sack of despair they carry
need to unload some of it

excrement of hate
guilt and fear
they throw at the world in general
but aiming with precision at me

the teflon cloak I wear usually protects

but they are cunning
salvating
waiting in ambush
for a button to become undone

You are where I go
should some of it stick
the shadows disappear

You are where I go
when their harsh words
leave a stain of self-doubt

You are where I go
to wash it clean

encourage me to unravel timid wings
in flight towards your laughter

Destination   Safe

You are where I go

Angel Wings

for Tina

It is the 18th day of the 14th year
a 15-year-old girl is dead
police found her floating in the water
a plastic bag wrapped around her head

the water is Red
the blood of hatred
the River filled with tears
the news breaks my heart
and takes me back
to my own youth
too many similarities

How many times was I struck in the face?
Go back where you came from squaw
15 years old then too

harsh fists
he could have killed me
and he probably would have
if he thought he could get away with it
there were witnesses

but not one stepped up to say
Enough!
Stop!

in their silence
they condone

so now 36 years later
on this 18th day
and a 15-year-old girl is dead

no one stands silent
No! No More!
Sisters speak out
our voices awaken the Land

and for our beautiful young Angel?
spread your wings
you will hear hateful words
no more

Tamra

I never knew you
other than to know
you have gone away
your story came on the news
again yesterday

I am sad for your Mom
 I held my own newborn baby
and made a promise

I will do my best for you – honest

I promise to fill your heart with a pride
our people have known for years
I will love you through
mess and pain and tears
love you for
happiness, triumph, courage
and for being so strong

What happened to Tamra
was terribly wrong
Who was there to protect her?
No one on that day

but that does not give my foster mom
any right to say

Tamra's Mom probably sold her
for a bottle of wine
to go partying
those Indians
happens all the time

What the hell was she thinking?
That I would agree?

Instead
it provides a moment of clarity

Realizing   she has puked out lie after lie like this
all my young life
filled with hatred   contempt
bitterness and strife

She says that my people are nothing more
than a sad sorry lot
hateful words
I carry and never forgot

She is so   hateful   sad   wrong

my people rise
every time
even when beaten down
I know we are strong
it makes me proud to be brown

So go back where you came from
faux mom
take your old ideas too
I refuse to listen
to anymore lies told by you

As for Tamra
we care   love you
and hope you will come
(or came)
Home

none of us
ever need feel that we are alone

Secrets

Taking innocence
without regard

has someone done the same to you?
who?

Just a child
laughing with glee
moments before ambush
when you stole
a gift from me

Dark and ugly
is how I felt
under the stairs
where I knelt

How sad a crime has been committed
unspeakable acts
but no one notices
hidden

I was just a child
unable to talk

and even today
it is a difficult walk

to admit
being harmed
in a place
that everyone thought
I would be safe

WIHTIKOW (*abandonment*)

a dark force that influences
causes harm
will consume — if allowed to do so

Sickness

Hate
permeates

runs through the veins like vinegar
laced with coarse sand

too many slaps across the head
causes brain damage
as in breaking   will   confidence   hope

words pierce
stupid son-of-a-bitch

Contemptuous foster child   you are told

Your biological mother died in winter
home-made 100-proof and frozen limbs

No one ever asked what drove her to that end?

Outcome?
A child alone
and in despair

that sets off a chain reaction

kick the dog   throw rocks at the pigs
tear out prized Azaleas
then blame it on the raccoons

the little masked bastards that travel under cover of darkness

Little bastards
That's what they called us

Water Generously

Parched Earth
has not rained
cannot remember the last time

Cracks

cries from those things
that would have grown

promise of things
that will never be

Ruins

the shadow of things
that once were

Erosion
hostile environment
requires healing and care

Parched love
the same
but for
the feather of hope
gently landing
in places
in need of magic

Slow Death

I'm going to do whatever I have to do
to make this marriage work
he says
just before turning on the tv and turning all his attention
to yet another documentary
one he's probably seen before
twice

Don't ever stop dating your wife
they say
so he takes the advice and we go to the pow wow
all the while he is texting with other women
has told them they are beautiful

how did he kill beauty?
why did I let him?

but it isn't supposed to bother me
that he has female
friends
I'm insecure he says
it's no wonder I don't want to go out in public
with you

But who can blame him?
our conversations
mundane
the dog
how much for the power bill
who took out the garbage

Things I say that matter me
he doesn't hear
just nods
then months later
asks me my opinion on what was just said

Want to go for a walk?
too tired
always
except when the boys call to go for a game of golf
he can get up at 5 a.m. and go all day
coming home to ask
what's for dinner?

Corpse

They are holding her funeral today
even though she has been dead for years

her body walked around
her mouth
spewing the same filth that killed her spirit

Nobody cares about Nelson Mandela's funeral, why don't they show
  something else on the TV?

I don't give to the Food Bank because those people should be buying their
  own food for their kids instead of spending it on booze all the time.

I am sick of hearing about this Idle No More nonsense, all those people
  ever do is hold out their hands and beg and take and beg.

Six days a week
cursing the Universe
repenting on Sunday
attending a church service
then beginning the tirade again
after making communion without a guilty conscience

did she even notice the beauty of a sunrise?
choosing instead to

spread poison
pulling out wild flowers by the root

That is what killed her
not old age
just old and poisonous ideas

Dulling

Hand me another glass of wine
an old and melancholy friend
Merlot
full-bodied conversations with him
are the only way to stop thoughts of you
so I think
depends how much I drink

Two glasses
I am still okay with being alone
four
makes me want to pick up the phone

I spill some on the counter
wipe it away
that sixth drink
I no longer think
tuning out life's most precious emotion

Love

Until the morning comes
the preoccupation begins anew
it always does

Phoney

No clean-shave here
you need those whiskers
to hold on that mask

the one
reserved for the boys

that mask helps you perform
on cue and contrived
joke after joke

And they laugh
those boys
but your family does not

I am not the least bit surprised

I saw you with them tonight
you did not wear the mask
no need
no audience

So to your wife and daughter
you offered only
grey skin   laden with frown-lines

You call this
a family dinner?

I watch
as you sit
and text
ignoring your family

I watch
as you close your eyes
take a nap
right there at the table

Your wife
invisible
a piece of lint
to be brushed away

But the mask goes on again
when your cell phone rings

It is the boys
at the other end of the line
treated to joke after joke
and your wife?

sits across from you
naked and in pain
poking tasteless food with a fork

You are sad and phoney
everyone sees it
but no one says it

Why?

Trolls

Yes
talking about you

Doomed from the start
your black heart
disguised
through the haze
caused by wine

Your gruesome expression
as deep as dark sin
lighten up
with one sip that led to
too many more

Before you know it
we are on the floor
a date rape I suppose you would call it

I have been wandering along too long
being alone for too long
causes bad choices
take you as my lover
until it is clear you are a swine

on your computer
an open screen
I wasn't supposed to see

Looking for *casual anal sex*

with this
it is over now
I say hurrah
the first image of you
gruesome   what I saw
that one is true

Damn that wine
attracting trolls

Warning Label

You ought to come with a warning

that looking into your eyes
as wonderfully blue as the Prairie sky
might result in wishing for forever
when really it is just this moment that counts

You ought to come with a warning

that the feel of your skin against mine
would leave a craving greater
than the need for water and wine
a hunger
satisfied only by your caress
now I await anorexic distress

You ought to come with a warning

that I would be reminded
to feel
to desire
to love
but a one-sided thing
a cut-out paper doll
a play thing
a fling

You ought to come with a warning

that there is an expiry date too
one night only
still
I am glad it was you

But now I am left wondering
what that says about me?

to need a warning label
in order to see?

Costume

Winning first prize
causes shame
that someone thought it is alright
to dress me up like a little Indian
at Halloween

Parading me out there with all the other ghouls and vampires
    and monsters
laughing at me and pointing fingers

wearing an itchy gunny-sack
some cheap feathers
and they braided my hair

when the comments of savage and little squaw start to wane
someone hands me an envelope
a one-dollar bill

later that day
hiding in the bathroom
steel wool is used
to scrub off the brown

it still scars

Indian Bar

I like being in an Indian Bar
everywhere you look
brown skin
black hair
some of those Indians wear tattoos
given to them
by their brothers in prison
a badge of some sort
or just a reminder
of the turmoil they have lived through

I like Indian Bars
the people are honest
they come here to drink
and they never ask
so, what do you do for a living?
like that is the only measure of worth

They want to know where you are from
says a lot more

Tonight I am with my Inuit friend
the light that is a constant
north of 60
has arrived for the season
it shines in her eyes all year

But some have let their light go dim
drowing it in this Indian Bar
with beer   cheap cigarettes   and gin

Like that artist who is sitting over there
in the shadows
as though a dark corner is enough
to hide his shame

A thin veil of carving dust
is in his hair
and on his clothes
signalling that this is how he rages
carving raw beauty
telling stories of strength
but never speaking them aloud
it is tiresome to explain
for those who do not feed their spirit

So he does not talk
except for his eyes
which are sad and frustrated

What is behind them
fights to get out
in his art
and it is strong
even the haze and darkness in this Indian Bar
cannot silence

Now I see a woman
singing and laughing
she is happy to be here at this Indian Bar

A glass of beer
tequila shooter
lemon
you would call her heavy   I suppose
but her teeth are shiny and white
her laugh is a roar

She is safe here in this Indian Bar
away from the man who slaps her

He is passed out at home
so she sneaks away
wearing sunglasses
to hide the bruises on her face
or maybe the bruises to her spirit

She likes it here in this Indian Bar
forgetting him
by pressing her body
against someone
who does not make a fist

She is defiant
and will be fine
telling herself
this is the last time

she will sit here at this Indian Bar

And I will leave too
not liking what is built here
feeding sadness
with spirits that come in a bottle

Fine brewers since 1934
that was the year of the Great Depression
still is for some

I will leave
but never be ashamed
of those who stay

They have their reasons

for them
I pray

Thunder

The sound of thunder
a song of you

heavy droplets of rain cleanse
the first night our spirits join
Old Ones sing love songs
resonating in the voice of thunder

this storm will pass
leaving a magnificent rainbow in its wake
etched on my soul
alive in memory

the storm washes away
parched residue
which has been gathering in corners for too long

a necessary storm
that brings warmth
and knowledge

Goddess has been listening to my prayers
even so
the sound of thunder
passes too quickly

Pink Satin Flowers

Sewing pink satin flowers
on an old ragged dress
trying to make it look new

sew purple lace along the hem
the needle pricks my finger
it bleeds
but I keep on sewing

attach an old patch from my old Brownie hat
too-wit   too-woo
brings a fleeting smile

hands keeping busy
in an attempt to stop
from calling

still no message

a chocolate cake recipe
that is deliciously sinful
is worth a try

start collecting the baking ingredients
then stop short

eating a whole cake alone

only adds to cellulite
more unnecessary baggage

already enough of that

Go for long walk instead
let the wind run his fingers
through uncombed hair

Purposely force mind to childhood memories
then buy an orange popsicle at the corner store
letting it melt to cause sticky fingers

do not want that on the telephone receiver
still
no message

I see a pile of books that want to be read
so I will
and travel within the imagination of someone
who is not me

it is probably safer there

Take a spoonful of peanut butter for my supper
make lemonade
allowing the sting of fresh juice

to run over the pin prick
still sensitive on my finger

these few moments of pain will pass

the other?
That will take some time

Until then
I continue to wear this old ragged dress
looking around for some other piece of clothing
on which to sew more
pink satin flowers

Black Dog

Slummin' it I see?
refers to me

Normalized dysfunction
even he can make me feel small
taught to believe that our women
have no worth at all

it is how we get in to trouble
not with the law
trouble with deciphering all the rotten things we saw
or did
bad decisions just to fit in

so
before you ask her why she did not leave?
ask him
why he hit her?
putting the heart of a woman
on the ground

violating the teachings
old and sacred

HE DOG, Oglala Sioux: *It is well to be good to women in the strength of our manhood because we must sit under their hands at both ends of our lives.*

Nechi Agin Monias (*my friend the white man*)

Why do defensive?
I am not your Kookum who says

She's okay, I guess, for a white girl

Nor am I your mother
who prayed for a certain type of grandchild

 I am not your uncle who whispers

It's alright to date one,
but why'd you have to marry her?

I am your friend
and I will not cast judgement
except to say
I cannot imagine being with anyone
who does not dance

That's all

Four-Leggeds Speaking

When hearts erode
like dried up top soil
humanity ceases to grow

Too many times
when I go outside
I hear the coyotes cry

It is 5 in the afternoon
too early for their song
it is like they are praying
or maybe saying
what are you doing?

They plan to dig up the land
change the whole valley too

coyotes will be homeless
(humans too?)
where will coyote babies go?

Fast Forward

A single mom of 3
she could take another part-time job

but when would she see her babies?
Rents will soar
when they dig up the land
worshipping a new golden calf

money   money   money   money
(laugh)

Somewhere
humanity got buried

Creator is watching

it must be a test
that we are failing

humanity
needs to be more than just a concept or word

pray for rain

Lament and Repent

Attempting to banish dark feelings
keep those bandaids
from falling
frayed at the edges and threatening to let go

little pieces of memory
hanging onto guilt

forces ruminants
what is forgiveness?

Only knowing
it is something I must do

I no longer speak with that woman
took me in as a child
treated like a stray
she disappeared with the years

what does it mean
that I shed no tears?

Worn down
after years of being
the only one who writes?
visits?

makes telephone calls?
yes
tired of trying and trying   to glue together shattered bits

which have become too fragmented and chipped
for any sort of reconstruction

maybe it was always that way
and I just could not see it
or
did not want to

I lived in a haze

until that day I met a man with a braid
spoke Cree
and said to me
you should learn

but I think he meant more
than just learning about the Nehiyaw
he meant
learn to honour both worlds

so I must honour that woman
and her shortcomings
and others like her
and will try to forgive

taking the Indian out of the child

because now   I am a Mother too
and I take back that little one
nurturing   teaching
healing wounds
with love   forgiveness   and prayer

KOOKUM (*spirit wisdom*)

*our journey and how we choose to experience it
depends on our understanding of self
wise one
revered Elder of the circle*

Lilly

I never fully understood the teachings of Jesus Christ
until I met an Old Woman
four foot ten
reminds me of Yoda
and just as wise

She has never been sentenced to jail
but she has done hard time
beaten to the point of death in Residential School
internal bleeding
the nuns did not send her to hospital until the next day

There
she lay in a coma
for eleven months

But she does not dwell on it
will not empower those early years
fraught with a litany of woe
peppered with hate
a mix of fear

She will not allow it to hinder her growth
towards becoming
the Old Woman who stands here

proud
strong
courageous

Too many now rely on her strength
which has become their starting place
of a shared sacred space
because of this Old Woman

who
years ago
accepted the unspeakable pain that arrived
when her young husband passed too soon

It was then two voices showed up
both promising something.

Spirits
which come in a bottle
and the Spirits
of the Old Voices we hear in the wind

Her husband is gone
their love remains
so she promises
to never drown those memories
but to keep their love   alive and powerful
honouring the memory of her husband
by honouring Spirit   The Old Ones

Transformation
smudging with sage   sweetgrass   cedar
she offers prayers for her children
for all children
and a promise that she will embrace
the rhythm of life
no matter what it may bring

It leads her to the circle
that magic place
peaceful place   the church forbade
for no good reason

Triumphant
Old Woman stands with an Eagle feather fan
held high at the honour beat
in a dance honouring her

Creator knows
she has earned the respect
towards her role as an Elder
as she continues to beckon
influence
encourage as many as she can
back to the dance

ancient
but new to those who have been disconnected
as she once was
but is no more

It is going on now   3 generations
this dance
getting stronger
and happening
because she let go of pain
felt it
but let it die
remembering instead   the love
a heart so large
it caused rebirth
resurrecting with it
traditions
the Old Ways
and extending that knowledge to her children
grandchildren   great grandchildren   all of Creator's children

Determined
they will not suffer the same
pain
disconnection
wandering in darkness

that was a long time ago

Sweetgrass, Sage and Cedar

Witches
devils
darkness and filth
Nothing good can come from those who worship rocks
we call her Mother Earth

sinners
soulless
destined to doom
searching for truth without any room
for light

I almost faint
the first time visiting a real Indian Medicine Man
do not know what to expect

will he have a bone piercing through his nose?
Witch doctor
will he bite the head off a chicken or snake?
summon the despicable?

He sets herbs on fire in some type of sea shell
then tells me to smudge
it scares me
I do not know what that means

Is he casting a spell that will lead to dancing naked
 and being covered in blood?
childhood voices
things I was told
warned about
savages

Until he explains
the smoke carries your prayers up to Creator
very similar to when Catholics burn their incense at Easter

Tentative   I reach out
cradling   welcoming   reconnecting
old memories from the shadows
mine now
I smudge

sweetgrass
sage
cedar

something finally awakes
and my heart breaks
at knowing I just shared something
ancient and strong

a starting point
towards where I belong

Twisted

Amy
today she is having trouble with her teenage daughter
yesterday   trouble with her ex
the day before   trouble at her work
the garden she plants will not grow

Where is the respite?

Some say that Amy is the name of a fallen angel
   who is the president in hell
others say the name comes from the Latin which means Beloved

whichever the case   Amy needs a break today
bring on the be loved every now and then   eh?
tucking in and crawling under a warm starblanket
she prays

a flash of lightning wakes her at midnight
electrical and fierce
its sheets emblazon the sky
this latest storm was not unexpected

just two hours ago the television was on
her hearing not as sharp anymore
so the volume is turned high

weatherman says a wild system coming in
low pressure from the southwest
isolated supercells
updrafts
producing
damaging wind
large hail
tornados

Supercells like cancer cells
moving swiftly and erratically
taking on a life of their own
solely for the purposes of destruction

Supercells
in part   a description of Amy's life
she prays for a sunny day
faith
snuggling comfort under the starblanket

a new beginning

Red

Red is the man
Blue the colour of my heart
pulsating veins carrying memories

They fuel
I feel
I create   havoc
                  illusion

Red man
paint my heart blue with memories
still warm and nourishing

Places
where I can go no more

Hearing the Earth

Spreading heart-shaped stones along the pathway
where she walks
knowing each time she sees the stones
thoughts turn to him

He sings love songs and prayer songs
hoping they carry on the wind

He dreams of laughter and love
things she will give him

but he is afraid to ask

He has fallen before
it left a scar

She did not cause it
but is punished anyway

She is everywhere
but in his arms

He has to open them

Recurring Feature

Always scattered
never landing

a loose thread
causes a loss of balance
roaming in search of safety and identity
open to criticism undeserved
searching for light
tender and kind
I come in to your arms
cherishing the warmth

You Know Who You Are

This one is for you
who sits in judgement
will never take a drink of wine in celebration
because
I do not want to be like them
Dirty drunken Indians
that wretched.chorus

Shed that cloak of shame
Them is you
always was
your skin is brown too

Those white people who surround you
talk behind your back
a well-behaved Uncle Tom

forever acting
you will never belong
anywhere

So wake up and join the song
the drum dance
a first step
in righting the wrong
that still has too strong of a grip   on your heart

If the Heavens

If the Heavens collapse at this very moment
and I   caught in the middle
would fall
like I did for you

Swallowed in euphoria
where might I land?
Will you save me?

If the Heavens collapse
and I died today
I would say thank you

For stopping the pain
for ending the longing
but mostly
for finding the love

I have waited too long for someone
who does not feel the need to hit me
literally and metaphorically

If the Heavens should fall
(*Book of Revelations – Book of my Life*)

I am ready
because you finally showed up

now it matters not
how many storms I had to endure

From this day forward
it shall simply be called
a bit of bad weather

Journey

So imperfect
wild and free
it is what makes you   *perfect for me*

These words you said
deep in your heart

and with that
for the first time   in my life
the right start

Water Toy Rental

Wanna play with me?
would have said it
just like that
had we met
40 years earlier

Floating on an inner tube
sharing a freezie
orange
I would have let you
pull my pigtails

And it would have been
love at first sight
because
that is how it happened for real

Departures

I can't stand all that noise.

is what she says
but what it means is
I do not want to be around all those Indians

her way of saying
I ain't coming to your wedding

I used to refer to her as my mother
now we do not even talk
after she spurned
You are having a Traditional ceremony?
Yes that means there will be drums

she will not come to my wedding
because drums are too loud?
and
I am marrying a Cree

tall and handsome
with features that make no mistake about culture

so of course
I understand
she will not come to my wedding

because
I never could understand
all her noise either
Indians are bad

I like this silence
and this dance
sometimes upheaval is good

I Am Proud

Perhaps it is just me
but I can never figure out
why it is deplorable for a monias (white guy) to say mean things
but if a neechie (Indian guy) tells you a bald-faced lie
people believe and follow
as if it were gospel?

Like that Hoop Dancer who forbade me
and lied
you are never supposed to dance
because you grew up with the monias
you do not know how to show the proper respect
so you are not allowed to dance
ever

It broke my heart and I cried
and what was my point of reference
on whether what he said was true
or just mean-spirited?
I didn't know any others   brown
I had been to only one pow wow

was so moved
called by the drum
something deep inside awoke and I cried then too
tears of joy   overwhelmed
as hundreds of the blessed moved

in harmony
in rhythm
with purpose and pride
feathers   ribbons   beads

so close to me
I could smell the smoke tan

I had no moccasins
but my dreams of belonging
crushed
at being told I am disrespectful
You aren't allowed to dance
you are too white even if your skin is brown

like I had a choice to be raised away from my own people?
no
they tore me from my Mother's arms the very day I was born
ever since I have been searching for a home

I found it here in this song
in the dance
only to be told   I am wrong

A few years later
sitting in prayer with Mooshum
feeding my spirit with smudge
he can feel a sadness within me

there is a pow wow tomorrow
Mooshum will raise his Eagle feather at Grand Entry

What is troubling you   Little One?

The explanation had hidden herself   somewhere near my falsetto
reaching for the words
expressing my sorrow of what being a scooped kid means

I can never take part in the dance
I act too white
that is what I was told

Mooshum turns ashen
regaining his composure after reaching for an Eagle feather
loose
amongst   sage   tobacco   and coloured cloths
he hands me the feather

If you want to dance
then dance
anyone can dance
come back to the Circle
make yourself an outfit
and always promise yourself this

That never again will you ask permission   to be who you are

Mooshum
kisakihitin

Courage
it is the colour of the dress I now wear

Pow Wow Wow

Celebrating culture
celebrating you

Bologna and bannock
the sandwich special

you're special

Earrings with feathers
a reminder
that loving you
has allowed me to fly

Chicken dance
I long to slow dance with you

Gourmet lemonade   good
but not as refreshing
as a sweet smile from you

Neckbones   Indian tacos
I want your taco

Teepees
want to go creepin' with you .

Fancy dance bussel
reminds me
of the vibrant colours of you
and that time
moves too quickly

so let's dance
together

Bear Song

Creator this prayer is to you
thank you for this perfect and beautiful soul
who   through your grace and wisdom
has grown inside of me
and today he is born

Born with him
new hope
a renewal of pride
and promise

please help me to guide him
in strength and in love
that this little bear spirit
never feel the loneliness of being disconnected from oneself

I am here

Please help guide me
to the people
places
and things that are good
so that this little bear spirit will learn
the Old Ways
from those whose hearts radiate with
the teachings of the Old Ones

walking the Red Road
where shame   despair   and sadness shall never be worn

I pray that this little bear spirit
finds   strength   beauty   and love
in things no longer hidden
that were once in danger of being lost and forgotten

Creator help this little bear spirit walk gently in to his future

On this day
my promise to you both
I shall always be by your side
never abandoning
but always building upon
the things that allow us
to know the secrets towards magic

Amen

Blessings

I thank Creator for giving me
the ability to recognize the miracle
of everyday things

a quiltwork of memory
of beauty in the moment

dandelion rubs in the summer
snow face-wash in winter
joyous squeals of laughter

I watch my children do this

each time it happens these days
the more precious

the passage of time
happens too quickly
it will not be long before that playful honesty matures
childhood is so short

my heart is warmed by their imagination
which includes a cat dressed in doll clothes

ours is a musical
a comedy

a drama
a love story

yes   definitely a love story
with pronouncements of truth
like
I love bake sales!

makes me wonder
can life have a deeper meaning
than a really good peanut butter cookie?

so for today
I thank Creator for allowing me
to be a part of their world
watching beauty
joy and splendor unfold
with a sweet lump in my throat

Warm Embrace

I remember it clearly
soft wool
knitted by Kookum
pink   white   yellow
the image of a daisy in the centre of that blanket
that brought such warmth

age 5   and it was my Christmas present

I loved it
smelled like Kookum's house
a wood-burning stove
baking   fresh bannock and ginger snaps laced with pepper

it was with me always
that blanket

in the evening
watching television
hugging me
with the love and warmth Kookum made sure
was part of every purl

I took it to bed
and it became part of my dreams
a magic carpet

I carried it everywhere
for years and years

that blanket over my shoulders
helped me get through that thunderstorm
protecting me
offering comfort

I felt safe
under that blanket
a place I wanted to stay

That is why the feeling was so familiar
when I met you
and you put your arms around me
for the first time

Summer Stroll

A hot August noon
parched earth
leaves slowly turn
my love walks beside me
he is in the wind
that cools my face
I am with him
everywhere
all the time
Creator has shaped
these rocks for us both
affirming his blessing
for the path
we travel together
as one

Closer

The closer to you
moving further away
from irrational fears caused by others

Shifting
comfortably into
what I thought was a dream
but now
each day spent with you
is real

I have your love
all that is good
you give to me freely
always

The closer to you
layers of happiness
and warmth
swept into paradise
with never a fear of drowning

Uncovering the essence
purity and joy

The closer to you
the colours more vibrant

some I have never even seen before
moving across my face
soft as moss

That is what you did
taking what once was a rock
covering it with softness
so it is no longer a danger
mostly to itself

The closer to you
and I am whole
because I am safe
to show you my light
and darkness

Ever movement
always dance
abundance in life   love   laughter
no longer
left to chance

The closer to you

Red Road Singing

Creator
I thank you

for I   no longer listen
to voices of dread
implanted too early in my heart
and in my head

The seed of acceptance
I am starting to see
are lessons I learned
towards being me

The hard and the ugly
the big and the small
enlightenment   forgiveness   energy   time
I rejoice in it all

So now this pod
that you planted one day
will finally grow
walking the Red Road

It is where I shall stay

Hiy hiy

My Brown Skin

Kissed by the sunlight
kissed by God   Creator

my brown skin

the colour of the Earth
and bark on the trees
finally rooted
proud to be me

and in love
with my brown skin

Returning

At this kitchen table they laugh
my wonderful sisters
(*nimis*)
telling stories
pointing with their lips

one holds her tummy
while others press hand to lips
as if the sound will not escape

laughing   (*paapiwak*)

They talk about *old lead foot*
speeding from La to P.A.
in just over 2 hours   (it takes me 3)
or
how one night after wrapping moose meat in brown paper
(*nimis*) wakes up stiff and aching at midnight
so she dabs
sore bean junior
on her elbow
to help her get back to sleep
except she did not turn the light on

in the morning

blue dots all over her arm
(*paapiwak*)
Bingo dabber!

at this kitchen table
my eyes starting to produce tears
(*nimis*) thinks it is because
the laughing has tickled my face too hard
but that is only half true

I cry for real because
(*paapiwak*)
prompts vague memories buried in my cells
to remember

I cannot speak the language
yet

robbed by circumstance
but (*paapiwak*) my sisters and sitting at this kitchen table now
is my chance

and I embrace

ikwa meyo kisikaw

Acknowledgements

At the end of my life, should I be asked to list all of the people dear to me who have helped me in my journey, I'd be around another five years. lol.

Life is art and everything is poetry. I just happened to record a few of those moments in this manuscript. The painful moments recorded alongside the joy — and the joy in my life outweighs everything.

Kinanaskomitin to my Baby Bears: Jackson, Nahanni, and Daniel. I couldn't be more proud of how beautifully you have all grown and I know will continue to build.

Special thanks for inspiring me to Bernadette Wagner, Lorri Neilsen Glenn, Gregory A. Scofield, Lisa Bird-Wilson, Kenneth T. Williams, Sandra Topinka, Betty Sellers, James Misfeldt, Carol and Duane Wright, Eunice Cameron, Carol Draper, Kristin Teetaert, Krista Hannon, Lori Zak, Bev Jackson, Terry Boldt, Marilyn Robak, Colleen Marcotte, Joan Halberg-Mayer, Kathy Daley, Deb Whelan, Ashley Norton, Leonard Montgrand, Shelley Traves, Jenny Kriekle, Rose Gilks, Diane Ell, Kristin Catherwood, Caroline Reid, Brittany Reid, Ruth Barker, Joely BigEagle-Keequatooway, Tracey George Hesse, Cleone Chant, Silas White, John Kennedy, Neal McLeod, Stacey Fayant, Cristian Moya, Erik Mehlsen, Karlie King, Marc Proulx, Sharlene Holliday, Shannon Webb-Campbell, Feather Maracle Luke. Wind beneath my wings.

And my sisters and Gertie. You are so beautiful.

Also grateful for the love of my old Dad, Joe Adams, and my beloved Grandmother, Lena. And especially my beautiful childhood (and current) friend, Kathy Butler, and her mom, Blanche. You filled my beginnings with colour and love.

Thank you also to Luciana Ricciutelli and Renée Knapp at Inanna Publications.

Sending much gratitude as well to Saskatchewan Cultural Exchange, SaskCulture, Saskatchewan Arts Board, Saskatchewan Writers' Guild, and Canada Council for the Arts — all working to ensure our words and creativity are always a part of the landscape. Namaste.

Carol Rose Daniels is Cree and Dene with roots in Sandy Bay, northern Saskatchewan. She is a published novelist, poet, playwright, visual artist, and musician. She is the author of the award-winning novel *Bearskin Diary* (2015). A second novel, *Wapawikoscikanihk – The Narrows of Fear,* is forthcoming in 2018. As a visual artist, her work has been exhibited in art galleries across Saskatchewan and Northern Canada. As a musician, a CD of women's drum songs, in which Carol is featured, was recently nominated for a Prairie Music Award. Before pursuing her art on a full-time basis, Carol worked as a journalist for more than 30 years in television and radio at APTN, CTV, and CBC. She lives in Regina Beach.